To see a World in a Grain of Sand
And a Heaven in a Wild Flower
Hold Infinity in the palm of your hand
And Eternity in an hour.

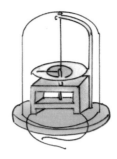

Henry Holt and Company, *Publishers since 1866*
Henry Holt® is a registered trademark of Macmillan Publishing Group, LLC.
175 Fifth Avenue, New York, NY 10010
mackids.com

Library of Congress Cataloging-in-Publication Data
Names: Demi.
Title: Marie Curie / Demi.
Description: New York : Henry Holt and Company, 2018 | Audience: Age 4-8.
Identifiers: LCCN 2017016323 | ISBN 9781627793896 (hardcover)
Subjects: LCSH: Curie, Marie, 1867–1934–Juvenile literature. | Curie, Pierre, 1859-1906–Juvenile literature. |
Women chemists–Poland–Biography–Juvenile literature. | Women chemists–France–Biography–Juvenile
literature. | Nobel Prize winners–Biography–Juvenile literature. | Radioactivity–History–Juvenile literature.
Classification: LCC QD22.C8 D46 2018 | DDC 540.92 [B]–dc23
LC record available at https://lccn.loc.gov/2017016323

Our books may be purchased in bulk for promotional, educational, or business use.
Please contact your local bookseller or the Macmillan Corporate and Premium Sales Department
at (800) 221-7945 ext. 5442 or by e-mail at MacmillanSpecialMarkets@macmillan.com.

First edition — 2018 / Designed by Gene Vosough
The artist used watercolor and mixed media to create the illustrations for this book.
Printed in China by RR Donnelley Asia Printing Solutions Ltd., Dongguan City, Guangdong Province

1 3 5 7 9 10 8 6 4 2

Marie Curie

DEMI

Henry Holt and Company
New York

On November 7, 1867, Maria Salomea Sklodowska was born at 16 Freta Street in Warsaw, Poland. Her family nicknamed her Manya. But one day, she would be known by another name: Marie Curie, one of the greatest scientists who ever lived.

Her mother was the principal of a school for girls, and her father was a math and physics teacher.

One of Manya's earliest memories was of her father's cabinet full of scientific instruments; Manya didn't know what the instruments were for, but they fascinated her.

Surrounded by three older sisters and a brother who all loved books, Manya figured out how to read at just four years old.

Manya loved to learn and was always at the top of her class,
even though she was two years younger than the other children.

Life in Poland was very difficult. Warsaw was occupied by Czarist Russia, and the Polish people had no freedom. Manya did all her lessons in Russian, but she also spoke fluent Polish and French.

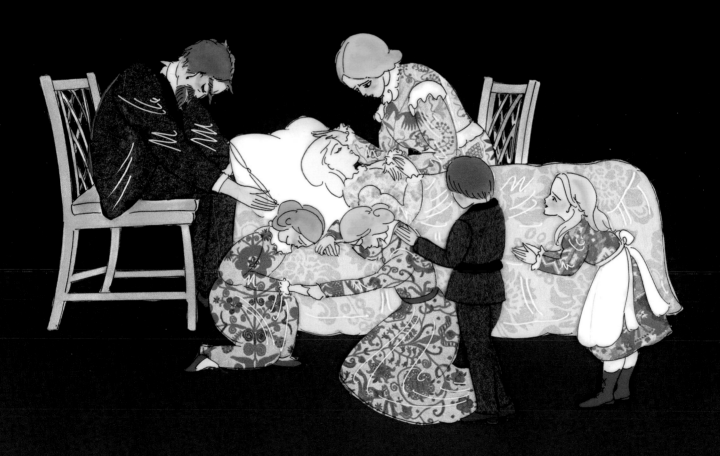

Life at home was also difficult. When Manya was eight, her eldest sister, Zosia, died of a disease called typhus. Just two years later, her mother died of tuberculosis, a lung disease. Manya began doing many of the jobs her mother had done at home, but she also started to work even harder on her lessons.

Because girls in Poland were not allowed to go to university, Manya and her sister Bronya wanted to study in Paris. But their family did not have enough money for them both to go.

The two sisters made a deal. Bronya would go to Paris to study medicine while Manya worked to support her. Then, after Bronya finished school, she would help Manya as Manya completed her studies.

In 1886 Manya worked as a governess to the children of a wealthy family who
owned a beet-sugar factory north of Warsaw. She also taught poor local children
to read and write.

On her own, Manya did not stop learning. She dreamed of Paris and the
Sorbonne, a famous university where she could attend formal classes, learn from
brilliant professors, and even use a laboratory for her experiments.

When Bronya completed her studies in 1890, she kept her promise to Manya. She became engaged to a fellow medical student and invited her youngest sister to live with them in Paris. But Manya decided that she preferred to live on her own. She came to Paris from Poland on a train ride that took forty hours.

In November of 1891, Manya enrolled at the Sorbonne as "Marie" Sklodowska. By this time, she had forgotten some of her French, and she didn't have very much money, but she was excited. Her dreams were finally coming true.

In 1893 she graduated first in her class, with an advanced degree in physics and a scholarship for the next year. In 1894 she graduated second in her class, with a degree in mathematics.

While completing these degrees, Marie met another brilliant mind. She was introduced to Pierre Curie by a friend and fellow Polish physicist. Pierre immediately recognized her intelligence. Marie was impressed by his work.

Pierre and his brother, Jacques, had made important discoveries while studying electricity, magnetism, heat, and crystals. Together they invented the electrometer, an instrument that measures electricity given off by crystals and other types of matter. Their ideas are used today in mobile phones, quartz watches, and record players.

Although Pierre was much older than Marie, they fell in love and were married in 1895. They celebrated by bicycling through the French countryside. When they returned, Marie studied to become a teacher, and Pierre eventually became a professor in Paris.

Marie continued to research, run the household, cook, and clean, and in 1897 she gave birth to their daughter Irene. The new mother was busy, but that did not slow her down. Thankfully, Pierre's father came to help with the baby.

With a child at home, Marie needed a place to continue her experiments. At Pierre's School of Physics and Industrial Chemistry, there was a leaky old shed that was cold and damp. But it was empty, and it was hers.

There, Marie decided to study the mysterious energy given off by a metallic element called uranium. She began her research by looking for other things that gave off the same invisible rays. She soon found the element thorium did, too. Her research was so successful that Pierre left his work to join hers.

Marie now knew any solid matter that contained uranium or thorium gave off rays, but nobody knew the cause.

Marie decided to find out. She started by looking for something unseen—a new element unlike any other known to man.

A mineral called pitchblende contained both uranium and thorium, so the Curies ordered several tons to test Marie's theory. First, she ground the rock to powder and then dissolved it in acid over and over again to separate all of the different elements that made up the pitchblende.

After everything was finally removed, Marie and Pierre found that pitchblende gave off radiation much greater than could be explained by the remaining uranium.

Marie and Pierre realized they had discovered not one but two new elements! They called the first new metal polonium, in honor of Marie's homeland, Poland. The second element they called radium. They also created the word *radioactive* to describe substances that emitted rays or radiation.

Marie wrote about their findings, but other scientists were doubtful and demanded that the couple prove their results by figuring out the new elements' atomic weight.

For four years Marie and Pierre worked on this tricky problem. They removed all the known elements from the purified pitchblende until one day the only thing left was a tiny speck in a little glass container. They were not quite sure what to make of it.

In bed that night the two scientists tossed and turned, wondering if something had gone wrong.

Marie and Pierre decided that they couldn't sleep until they had figured it out. They headed back to the lab in the middle of the night.

It was pitch-black as they stumbled inside—except for one spot. There on the table, glowing in the darkness, was a tiny speck of light from Marie's little glass container.

The Curies finally had their pure radium!

Although they had managed to isolate only a tiny amount of radium, Marie was able to calculate its atomic weight.

They continued working in the old shed, but soon some interesting and painful problems arose. Although radiation from uranium had seemed harmless, radium was much, much stronger. Everything in the shed became radioactive. Marie and Pierre developed blisters and sores on their hands that would not heal for months. If they tried to carry a small tube of radium in a jacket pocket, it would burn their skin right through the glass and fabric.

They realized that radium's ability to burn skin might have a surprising use. If it could burn healthy flesh, it might also be able to burn away unhealthy parts. Parts that had cancer. Marie and Pierre had stumbled upon one of the greatest contributions to the world of modern medicine.

The year 1903 ended with the Curies receiving the most prestigious award of all: the Nobel Prize in Physics.

The following year, the Curies had their second daughter, Eve, and Pierre
accepted a job teaching at the Sorbonne.

Although Pierre began to feel weak, a hint at the unknown dangers of
radium, the hard work and research seemed to be paying off. The growing
family was happy.

On Thursday, April 19, 1906, everything changed.

It was a rainy afternoon when Pierre stepped out of a meeting with fellow professors. Not wanting to get too wet, he decided to run to his next appointment.

As he crossed the busy narrow street, Pierre accidentally stepped into traffic and was struck by a wagon, which killed him instantly.

Although Marie was devastated, she refused to let her sadness interfere with her work. Instead, she took over Pierre's classes and became the first female professor at the Sorbonne.

Marie continued her juggling act of teaching, researching, and caring for her daughters. She even found the time to prove once and for all that radium and polonium existed after Lord Kelvin, a British scientist, challenged her findings.

On November 7, 1911, Marie was awarded a second Nobel Prize, this time in chemistry, for the discovery of the elements radium and polonium. Marie traveled to Stockholm and received the medal from the king of Sweden himself, making her the first person to win the Nobel Prize twice.

Then in the summer of 1914, France went to war.
The German army began closing in on Paris, and
many soldiers were injured and dying.

Marie understood that X-raying soldiers quickly often meant the difference between
life and death. Marie had a truck turned into a mobile X-ray machine that could drive to
the wounded and X-ray them. Eventually she organized a fleet of twenty X-ray ambulances
called "Little Curies." By the end of World War I in 1918, more than one million wounded
men had been X-rayed thanks to Marie Curie.

For all of her work, Marie was invited to travel to America to accept a gram of radium worth $100,000 for her research. When she arrived in the spring of 1921, she received a hero's welcome and was honored at the White House by President Warren Harding.

Since its discovery, radium had become very popular. People drank it to cure arthritis, and companies put it in lipstick and face powder to make skin shine. Shampoo, soap, chocolate bars, and toothpaste all contained radium. The element was even painted on watches and aluminum airplane instruments to make them glow in the dark.

Female factory workers who painted these watches and instruments were called "Radium Girls."

As they painted, they would moisten the tips of their brushes in their mouths again and again to keep a very fine point. Some of the girls painted their teeth and fingernails with the glowing paint for fun. But eventually the girls began to notice that when they sneezed into their handkerchiefs, their handkerchiefs glowed in the dark.

Then they started to lose their teeth. They had accidentally poisoned themselves with radium.

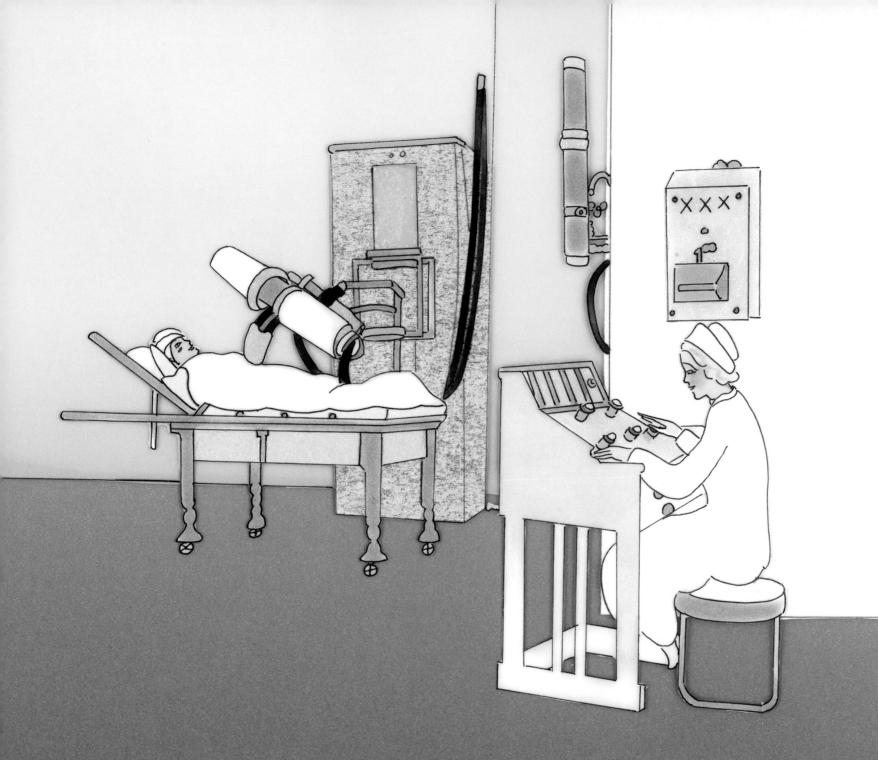

By the mid-1920s, scientists recognized the dangers of radioactivity. They realized that radiation given off from radium could both kill and cure. Although scientists began using protection when working with radiation, Marie had already started to become ill from all her years of exposure. On July 4, 1934, Marie Curie died in the French Alps at the age of 66.

Marie Curie's tireless research came at great cost, but her discoveries also greatly improved life: She and her husband had successfully developed a new weapon in the fight against cancer, and Marie's ideas about the atom helped her daughter Irene unlock the power of nuclear energy.

Marie was convinced that humanity would draw more good than evil from new discoveries. And so, throughout her life's work, she never hesitated in the pursuit of knowledge.

✳ TIMELINE ✳

NOVEMBER 7, 1867: Maria Salomea Sklodowska is born in Warsaw, Poland.

1869: Chemist and inventor Dmitri Mendeleev creates the Periodic Table of the Elements in an attempt to categorize the elements based on their atomic weights. Through discrepancies he discovers among these weights, he is able to predict the existence of new elements yet to be identified and leaves space for them on his table.

1883: Marie graduates from high school.

1890–91: Marie attends the "Flying University," an illegal school notable for accepting female students and for promoting Polish nationalism in spite of Russian occupation. She studies chemistry at the Museum of Industry and Agriculture in a laboratory run by her cousin, Jozef Boguski, who formerly worked with Dmitri Mendeleev.

SEPTEMBER 1891: Marie moves to Paris to attend the university at the Sorbonne.

1893: Marie graduates from the Sorbonne with a master's degree in physics. She earns a second degree a year later, this time in mathematics.

JULY 26, 1895: Marie marries Pierre Curie.

1895: Wilhelm Roentgen discovers X-rays and provides new insights into what will become the study of radiology.

1896: Henri Becquerel discovers uranium radiation (Becquerel rays), which inspires Marie's doctoral work.

1898: Marie discovers polonium and radium and in the process coins the term *radioactivity*. It takes her nearly four years to isolate radium; she is never able to fully isolate polonium.

JUNE 1903: Marie becomes the first woman in Europe to earn a doctorate in science.

1903: Marie, Pierre, and Henri Becquerel win the Nobel Prize in Physics for their research on Becquerel rays. It is the first time a woman has ever received this honor.

APRIL 19, 1906: Pierre is killed in a traffic accident. Marie takes over his teaching position at the Sorbonne, becoming the university's first female professor.

1911: Responding to a challenge to her theories on radiation presented by Lord Kelvin, Marie confirms radium's status as an element, thus earning it a place on the Periodic Table. Marie wins a Nobel Prize in Chemistry for her discovery of polonium and radium, making her the first person ever to win two Nobel Prizes.

1914: Marie creates the Radium Institute in Paris to serve as a center for scientific study.

JUNE 28, 1914: The assassination of Archduke Franz Ferdinand of Austria-Hungary leads to World War I. On August 3, France joins the war. Marie is appointed director of the Red Cross Radiology Service and sets up a fleet of mobile radiology labs, later dubbed *Petites Curies* (Little Curies). Her daughter Irene travels with her to the war front to help treat wounded soldiers.

1921: Marie tours the United States, where she receives many honorary degrees, meets President Warren Harding, and is given a gram of radium for her laboratory. She returns to the States a second time in 1929.

JULY 4, 1934: Marie dies of leukemia at the age of 66.

✳ GLOSSARY ✳

ATOM — the smallest unit of a substance and a basic building block of molecules

ATOMIC WEIGHT OR RELATIVE ATOMIC MASS — a ratio of an atom's mass relative to that of carbon, one of the most commonly occurring elements on Earth

CHEMISTRY — the science that deals with substances and their transformations

ELEMENT — the simplest substance made up of atoms; it cannot be broken down any further

MINERAL — a naturally occurring substance, such as a rock, usually found in the ground

NOBEL PRIZE — an annual award created by the Swedish inventor Alfred Nobel; it can be given for accomplishments in chemistry, literature, peace, physics, physiology, or medicine

NUCLEAR ENERGY — the energy stored in the very center of an atom

PHYSICS — the science of matter and energy

PITCHBLENDE — a radioactive black mineral

POLONIUM — a radioactive metallic element

RADIATION — energy that moves from one place to another such as light, sound, heat, and X-rays

RADIOACTIVITY — the process of an atom losing energy by giving off rays

RADIUM — a very radioactive metallic element that creates a green glow

THORIUM — a metallic element; weakly radioactive

URANIUM — a chemical element; weakly radioactive

✳ FURTHER READING ✳

Krull, Kathleen, and Boris Kulikov. *Marie Curie*. Giants of Science. New York: Puffin Books, 2007.

"Marie Curie—Biographical." Nobelprize.org. From *Nobel Lectures, Physics 1901-1921*. Amsterdam: Elsevier Publishing Co., 1967. https://www.nobelprize.org/nobel_prizes/physics/laureates/1903/marie-curie-bio.html.

"Mme. Curie Is Dead; Martyr to Science." *The New York Times*. November 3, 2010. http://www.nytimes.com/learning/general/onthisday/bday/1107.html.

Mortensen, Lori, and Susan M. Jaekel. *Marie Curie: Prize-Winning Scientist*. Minneapolis, MN: Picture Window Books, 2008.

Stine, Megan, and Ted Hammond. *Who Was Marie Curie?* New York: Grosset & Dunlap, an Imprint of Penguin Group (USA) LLC, 2014.